AGAINST THE GALILEANS

Julian the Apostate
Emperor of Rome

Translated: Wilmer Cave Wright
Edited by: D.P. Curtin

Dalcassian Publishing Co.
Philadelphia, PA

Against the Galileans

Library of Congress Cataloging-in-Publication Data

Copyright © 2018 Dalcassian Publishing Co.
In association with St. Macartan Press

Introduction

Julian, like Epictetus, always calls the Christians Galilaeans[1] because he wishes to emphasise that this was a local creed, "the creed of fishermen," and perhaps to remind his readers that "out of Galilee ariseth no prophet";[2] with the same intention he calls Christ "the Nazarene."[3] His chief aim in the treatise was to show that there is no evidence in the Old Testament for the idea of Christianity, so that the Christians have no right to regard their teaching as a development of Judaism. His attitude throughout is that of a philosopher who rejects the claims of one small sect to have set up a universal religion. He speaks with respect of the God of the Hebrews, admires the Jewish discipline, their sacrifices and their prohibition of certain foods, plays off the Jews against the Christians, and reproaches the latter for having abandoned the Mosaic law; but he contrasts the jealous, exclusive "particular" (μερικός) Hebraic God with the universal Hellenic gods who do not confine their attentions to a small and unimportant portion of the world. Throughout Julian's works there are scattered references, nearly always disdainful, to the Galilaeans, but his formal attack on their creed and on the inconsistencies of the Scriptures, which he had promised in *Letter* 55, *To Photinus*, the heretic, was not given to the general public, for whom he says he intends it, till he had left Antioch on his march to Persia in the early spring of 363. He probably compiled it at Antioch in the preceding winter.[4] Perhaps it was never completed, for at the time Julian had many things on his mind. It was written in three Books, but the fragments preserved are almost entirely from Book I. In the fifth century Cyril of Alexandria regarded the treatise as peculiarly dangerous, and said that it had shaken many believers. He undertook to refute it in a polemic of which about half survives, and from the quotations of Julian in Cyril's work Neumann has skilfully reconstructed considerable portions of the treatise. Cyril had rearranged Julian's hurriedly written polemic, in order to avoid repetitions and to bring similar subjects together. Moreover, he says that he omitted invectives against Christ and such matter as might contaminate the minds of Christians. We have seen that a similar mutilation of the letters occurred for similar reasons.

Julian's arguments against the Christian doctrine do not greatly differ from those used in the second century by Celsus, and by Porphyry in the third; but his tone is more like that of Celsus, for he and Celsus were alike in being embittered opponents of the Christian religion, which Porphyry was not. Those engaged in this sort of controversy use the same weapons over and over again; Origen refutes Celsus, Cyril refutes Julian, in much the same terms. Both sides have had the education of sophists, possess the learning of their time, borrow freely from Plato, attack the rules or lack of rules of diet of the opponents' party, point out the inconsistencies in the rival creed, and ignore the weaknesses of their own.[5]

For his task Julian had been well equipped by his Christian teachers when he was interned at Macellum in Cappadocia, and he here repays them for the enforced studies of his boyhood, when his naturally pagan soul rebelled against the Christian ritual in which he had to take part. In spite of his insistence on the inconsistency of the Christians in setting up a Trinity in place of the monotheism of Moses and the prophets, he feels the need of some figure in his own pantheon to balance that of Christ the Saviour, and uses, both in this treatise and in *Oration* 4, about Asclepius or Dionysus or Heracles almost the language of the Christians about Christ, setting these pagan figures up one after another as manifestations of the divine beneficence in making a link between the gods and mankind.

Though Julian borrowed from Porphyry's lost polemic in fifteen Books,[6] he does not discuss questions of the chronology and authorship of the Scriptures as Porphyry is known to have done. Libanius, always a blind admirer of Julian, says[7] that in this treatise the Emperor made the doctrines of the Christians look ridiculous, and that he was "wiser than the Tyrian old man," that is, Porphyry. But apparently the Christians of the next two centuries did not agree with Cyril as to the peculiarly dangerous character of Julian's invective. At any rate, the Council of Ephesus, in a decree dated 431, sentenced Porphyry's books to be burned, but did not mention Julian's; and again in a law of Theodosius II. in 448, Julian was ignored while Porphyry was condemned. When in 529 Justinian decreed that anti-Christian books were to be burned, Porphyry alone was named, though probably Julian was meant to be included. Not long after Julian's death his fellow-student at Athens, Gregory Nazianzen, wrote a long invective against him, in which he attacked the treatise Against the Galilaeans without making a formal refutation of Julian's arguments. Others in the fifth century, such as Theodoras of Mopsuestia and Philip Sideta, wrote refutations which are lost. But it was reserved for Cyril, Bishop of Alexandria, writing between 429 and 441, to compose a long and formal refutation of Julian's treatise; the latter seems to have been no longer in circulation, or was at least neglected, and Neumann thinks that the bishop was urged to write his polemic by his dislike of the heretical views of other and earlier antagonists of Julian, especially Theodorus of Mopsuestia. This refutation, which was dedicated to the Emperor Theodosius II, was in at least twenty Books. But for Cyril's quotations we should have a very vague idea of Julian's treatise, and as it is we are compelled to see it through the eyes of a hostile apologist. Cyril's own comments, and his summaries of portions of the treatise have been omitted from the following translation,[8] but the substance of the summaries has been given in the footnotes. The marginal numbers in the Greek text correspond with the pages of Spanheim's (1696) edition of Cyril's polemic *Pro Christiana Religione*, from which Neumann extracted and strung together Cyril's quotations of Julian. There is, therefore, an occasional lack of connection in Julian's arguments, taken apart from their context in Cyril's treatise.

Against the Galileans

Book I

39.[9] It is, I think, expedient to set forth to all mankind the reasons by which I was convinced that the fabrication of the Galilaeans is a fiction of men composed by wickedness. Though it has in it nothing divine, by making full use of that part of the soul which loves fable and is childish and foolish, it has induced men to believe that the monstrous tale is truth. **41.** Now since I intend to treat of all their first dogmas, as they call them, I wish to say in the first place that if my readers desire to try to refute me they must proceed as if they were in a court of law and not drag in irrelevant matter, or, as the saying is, bring counter-charges until they have defended their own views. **42.** For thus it will be better and clearer if, when they wish to censure any views of mine, they undertake that as a separate task, but when they are defending themselves against my censure, they bring no counter-charges.

It is worth while to recall in a few words whence and how we first arrived at a conception of God; next to compare what is said about the divine among the Hellenes and Hebrews; and finally to enquire of those who are neither Hellenes nor Jews, but belong to the sect of the Galilaeans, why they preferred the belief of the Jews to ours; and what, further, can be the reason why they do not even adhere to the Jewish beliefs but have abandoned them also and followed a way of their own. For they have not accepted a single admirable or important doctrine of those that are held either by us Hellenes or by the Hebrews who derived them from Moses; but from both religions they have gathered what has been engrafted like powers of evil, as it were, on these nations – **43.** atheism from the Jewish levity, and a sordid and slovenly way of living from our indolence and vulgarity; and they desire that this should be called the noblest worship of the gods.

52. Now that the human race possesses its knowledge of God by nature and not from teaching is proved to us first of all by the universal yearning for the divine that is in all men whether private persons or communities, whether considered as individuals or as races. For all of us, without being taught, have attained to a belief in some sort of divinity, though it is not easy for all men to know the precise truth about it, nor is it possible for those who do know it to tell it to all men. . . .[10] Surely, besides this conception which is common to all men, there is another also. I mean that we are all by nature so closely dependent on the heavens and the gods that are visible therein, that even if any man conceives of another god besides these, he in every case assigns to him the heavens as his dwelling-place; not that he thereby separates him from the earth, but he so to speak establishes the King of the All in the heavens[11] as in the most honourable place of all, and conceives of him as overseeing from there the affairs of this world.

69. What need have I to summon Hellenes and Hebrews as witnesses of this? There exists no man who does not stretch out his hands towards the heavens when he prays; and whether he swears by one god or several, if he has any notion at all of the divine, he turns heavenward. And it was very natural that men should feel thus. For since they observed that in what concerns the heavenly bodies there is no increase or diminution or mutability, and that they do not suffer any unregulated influence, but their movement is harmonious and their arrangement in concert; and that the illuminations of the moon are regulated, and that the risings and settings of the sun are regularly defined, and always at regularly defined seasons, they naturally conceived that the heaven is a god and the throne of a god.[12] For a being of that sort, since it is not subject to increase by addition, or to diminution by subtraction, and is stationed beyond all change due to alteration and mutability, is free from decay and generation, and inasmuch as it is immortal by nature and indestructible, it is pure from every sort of stain. Eternal and ever in movement, as we see, it travels in a circuit about the great Creator, whether it be impelled by a nobler and more divine soul that dwells therein, just as, I mean, our bodies are by the soul in us, or having received its motion from God Himself, it wheels in its boundless circuit, in an unceasing and eternal career.

44. Now it is true that the Hellenes invented their myths about the gods, incredible and monstrous stories. For they said that Kronos swallowed his children and then vomited them forth; and they even told of lawless unions, how Zeus had intercourse with his mother, and after having a child by her, married his own daughter,[13] or rather did not even marry her, but simply had intercourse with her and then handed her over to another.[14] **75.** Then too there is the legend that Dionysus was rent asunder and his limbs joined together again. This is the sort of thing described in the myths of the Hellenes. Compare with them the Jewish doctrine, how the garden was planted by God and Adam was fashioned by Him, and next, for Adam, woman came to be. For God said, "It is not good that the man should be alone. Let us make him an help meet like, him."[15] Yet so far was she from helping him at all that she deceived him, and was in part the cause of his and her own fall from their life of ease in the garden.

This is wholly fabulous. For is it probable that God did not know that the being he was creating as a help meet would prove to be not so much a blessing as a misfortune to him who received her? **86.** Again, what sort of language are we to say that the serpent used when he talked with Eve? Was it the language of human beings? And in what do such legends as these differ from the myths that were invented by the Hellenes? **89.** Moreover, is it not excessively strange that God should deny to the human beings whom he had fashioned the power to distinguish between good and evil? What could be more foolish than a being unable to distinguish good from bad? For it is evident that he would not avoid the latter, I mean things evil, nor would he strive after the former, I mean things good. And, in short, God refused to let man taste of wisdom, than which there could be nothing of more value for man. For that the power to distinguish between good and less good is the property of wisdom is evident surely even to the witless; **93.** so that the serpent was a benefactor rather than a destroyer of the human race. Furthermore, their God must be called envious. For when he saw that man had attained to a share of wisdom, that he might not, God said, taste of the tree of life, he cast him out of the garden, saying in so many words, "Behold, Adam has become as one of us, because he knows good from bad; and now let him not put forth his hand and take also of the tree of life and eat and thus live forever."[16] **94.** Accordingly, unless every one of these legends is a myth that involves some secret interpretation, as I indeed believe,[17] they are filled with many blasphemous sayings about God. For in the first place to be ignorant that she who was created as a help meet would be the cause of the fall; secondly to refuse the knowledge of good and bad, which knowledge alone seems to give coherence to the mind of man; and lastly to be jealous lest man should take of the tree of life and from mortal become immortal, – this is to be grudging and envious overmuch.

96. Next to consider the views that are correctly held by the Jews, and also those that our fathers handed down to us from the beginning. Our account has in it the immediate creator of this universe, as the following shows. . . .[18] Moses indeed has said nothing whatsoever about the gods who are superior to this creator, nay, he has not even ventured to say anything about the nature of the angels. But that they serve God he has asserted in many ways and often; but whether they were generated or un-generated, or whether they were generated by one god and appointed to serve another, or in some other way, he has nowhere said definitely. But he describes fully in what manner the heavens and the earth and all that therein is were set in order. In part, he says, God ordered them to be, such as light and the firmament, and in part, he says, God made them, such as the heavens and the earth, the sun and moon, and that all things which already existed but were hidden away for the time being, he separated, such as water, I mean, and dry land. But apart from these he did not venture to say a word about the generation or the making of the Spirit, but only this, "And the Spirit of God moved upon the face of the waters." But whether that spirit was ungenerated or had been generated he does not make at all clear.

49. Now, if you please, we will compare the utterance of Plato.[19] Observe then what he says about the creator, and what words he makes him speak at the time of the generation of the universe, in order that we may compare Plato's account of that generation with that of Moses. For in this way it will appear who was the nobler and who was more worthy of intercourse with God, Plato who paid homage to images, or he of whom the Scripture says that God spake with him mouth to mouth.[20] "In the beginning God created the heaven and the earth. And the earth was invisible and without form, and darkness was upon the face of the deep. And the spirit of God moved upon the face of the waters. And God said, Let there be light; and there was light. And God saw the light that it was good; and God divided the light from the darkness. And God called the light Day, and the darkness he called Night. And the evening and the morning were the first day. And God said, Let there be a firmament in the midst of the waters. And God called the firmament Heaven. And God said, Let the waters under the heaven be gathered together unto one place, and let the dry land appear; and it was so. And God said, Let the earth bring forth grass for fodder, and the fruit tree yielding fruit. And God said, Let there be lights in the firmament of the heaven that they may be for a light upon the earth. And God set them in the firmament of the heaven to rule over the day and over the night."[21]

In all this, you observe, Moses does not say that the deep was created by God, or the darkness or the waters. And yet, after saying concerning light that God ordered it to be, and it was, surely he ought to have gone on to speak of night also, and the deep and the waters. But of them he says not a word to imply that they were not already existing at all, though he often mentions them. Furthermore, he does not mention the birth or creation of the angels or in what manner they were brought into being, but deals only with the heavenly and earthly bodies. It follows that, according to Moses, God is the creator of nothing that is incorporeal, but is only the disposer of matter that already existed. For the words, "And the earth was invisible and without form" can only mean that he regards the wet and dry substance as the original matter and that he introduces God as the disposer of this matter.

57. Now on the other hand hear what Plato says about the universe: "Now the whole heaven or the universe, – or whatever other name would be most acceptable to it, so let it be named by us, – did it exist eternally, having no beginning of generation, or has it come into being starting from some beginning? It has come into being. For it can be seen and handled and has a body; and all such things are the objects of sensation, and such objects of sensation, being apprehensible by opinion with the aid of sensation are things that came into being, as we saw, and have been generated. . . [22] It follows, therefore, according to the reasonable theory, that we ought to affirm that this universe came into being as a living creature possessing soul and intelligence in very truth, both by the providence of God."[23]

Let us but compare them, point by point. What and what sort of speech does the god make in the account of Moses, and what the god in the account of Plato?

58. "And God said, Let us make man in our image, and our likeness; and let them have dominion over the fish of the sea, and over the fowl of the air, and over the cattle, and over all the earth, and over every creeping thing that creepeth upon the earth. So God created man, in the image of God created he him; male and female created he them, and said, Be fruitful and multiply and replenish the earth, and subdue it; and have dominion over the fish of the sea, and over the fowl of the air, and over all the cattle and over all the earth."[24]

Now, I say, hear also the speech which Plato puts in the mouth of the Artificer of the All.

"Gods of Gods! Those works whose artificer and father I am will abide indissoluble, so long as it is my will. Lo, all that hath been fastened may be loosed, yet to will to loose that which is harmonious and in good case were the act of an evil being. Wherefore, since ye have come into being, ye are not immortal or indissoluble altogether, nevertheless ye shall by no means be loosed or meet with the doom of death, since ye have found in my will a bond more mighty and more potent than those wherewith ye were bound when ye came into being. Now therefore hearken to the saying which I proclaim unto you: Three kinds of mortal beings still remain unborn, and unless these have birth the heaven will be incomplete. For it will not have within itself all the kinds of living things. Yet if these should come into being and receive a share of life at my hands they would become equal to gods. Therefore in order that they may be mortal, and that this All may be All in very truth, turn ye according to your nature to the contriving of living things, imitating my power even as I showed it in generating you. And such part of them as is fitted to receive the same name as the immortals, which is called divine and the power in them that governs all who are willing ever to follow justice and you, this part I, having sowed it and originated the same, will deliver to you. For the rest, do you, weaving the mortal with the immortal, contrive living beings and bring them to birth; then by giving them sustenance increase them, and when they perish receive them back again."[25]

65. But since ye are about to consider whether this is only a dream, do ye learn the meaning thereof. Plato gives the name gods to those that are visible, the sun and moon, the stars and the heavens, but these are only the likenesses of the invisible gods. The sun which is visible to our eyes is the likeness of the intelligible and invisible sun,[26] and again the moon which is visible to our eyes and every one of the stars are likenesses of the intelligible.[27] Accordingly Plato knows of those intelligible and invisible gods which are immanent in and coexist with the creator himself and were begotten and proceeded from him. Naturally, therefore, the creator in Plato's account says "gods" when he is addressing the invisible beings, and "of gods," meaning by this, evidently, the visible gods. And the common creator of both these is he who fashioned the heavens and the earth and the sea and the stars, and begat in the intelligible world the archetypes of these.

Observe then that what follows is well said also. "For," he says, "there remain three kinds of mortal things," meaning, evidently, human beings, animals and plants; for each one of these has been denned by its own peculiar definition. "Now," he goes on to say, "if each one of these also should come to exist by me, it would of necessity become immortal." And indeed, in the case of the intelligible gods and the visible universe, no other cause for their immortality exists than that they came into existence by the act of the creator. When, therefore, he says, "Such part of them as is immortal must needs be given to these by the creator," he means the reasoning soul. "For the rest," he says, "do ye weave mortal with immortal." It is therefore clear that the creative gods received from their father their creative power and so begat on earth all living things that are mortal. For if there were to be no difference between the heavens and mankind and animals too, by Zeus, and all the way down to the very tribe of creeping things and the little fish that swim in the sea, then there would have had to be one and the same creator for them all. But if there is a great gulf fixed between immortals and mortals, **66.** and this cannot become greater by addition or less by subtraction, nor can it be mixed with what is mortal and subject to fate, it follows that one set of gods were the creative cause of mortals, and another of immortals.

Accordingly, since Moses, as it seems, has failed also to give a complete account of the immediate creator of this universe, **99.** let us go on and set one against another the opinion of the Hebrews and that of our fathers about these nations.

Moses says that the creator of the universe chose out the Hebrew nation, that to that nation alone did he pay heed and cared for it, and he gives him charge of it alone. But how and by what sort of gods the other nations are governed he has said not a word, – unless indeed one should concede that he did assign to them the sun and moon.[28] However of this I shall speak a little later. Now I will only point out that Moses himself and the prophets who came after him and Jesus the Nazarene, yes and Paul also, who surpassed all the magicians and charlatans of every place and every time, **100.** assert that he is the God of Israel alone and of Judaea, and that the Jews are his chosen people. Listen to their own words, and first to the words of Moses: "And thou shalt say unto Pharaoh, Israel is my son, my firstborn. And I have said to thee, Let my people go that they may serve me. But thou didst refuse to let them go."[29] And a little later, "And they say unto him, The God of the Hebrews hath summoned us; we will go therefore three days' journey into the desert, that we may sacrifice unto the Lord our God."[30] And soon he speaks again in the same way, "The Lord the God of the Hebrews hath sent me unto thee, saying, Let my people go that they may serve me in the wilderness."[31]

106. But that from the beginning God cared only for the Jews and that He chose them out as his portion, has been clearly asserted not only by Moses and Jesus but by Paul as well; though in Paul's case this is strange. For according to circumstances he keeps changing his views about God, as the polypus changes its colours to match the rocks,[32] and now he insists that the Jews alone are God's portion, and then again, when he is trying to persuade the Hellenes to take sides with him, he says: "Do not think that he is the God of Jews only, but also of Gentiles: yea of Gentiles also."[33] Therefore it is fair to ask of Paul why God, if he was not the God of the Jews only but also of the Gentiles, sent the blessed gift of prophecy to the Jews in abundance and gave them Moses and the oil of anointing, and the prophets and the law and the incredible and monstrous elements in their myths? For you hear them crying aloud: "Man did eat angels' food."[34] And finally God sent unto them Jesus also, but unto us no prophet, no oil of anointing, no teacher, no herald to announce his love for man which should one day, though late, reach even unto us also. Nay he even looked on for myriads, or if you prefer, for thousands of years, while men in extreme ignorance served idols, as you call them, from where the sun rises to where he sets, yes and from North to South, save only that little tribe which less than two thousand years before had settled in one part of Palestine. For if he is the God of all of us alike, and the creator of all, why did he neglect us? **100.** Wherefore it is natural to think that the God of the Hebrews was not the begetter of the whole universe with lordship over the whole, but rather, as I said before, that he is confined within limits, and that since his empire has bounds we must conceive of him as only one of the crowd of other gods. **106.** Then are we to pay further heed to you because you or one of your stock imagined the God of the universe, though in any case you attained only to a bare conception of Him? Is not all this partiality? God, you say, is a jealous God. But why is he so jealous, even avenging the sins of the fathers on the children?[35]

115. But now consider our teaching in comparison with this of yours. Our writers say that the creator is the common father and king of all things, but that the other functions have been assigned by him to national gods of the peoples and gods that protect the cities; every one of whom administers his own department in accordance with his own nature. For since in the father all things are complete and all things are one, while in the separate deities one quality or another predominates, therefore Ares rules over the warlike nations, Athene over those that are wise as well as warlike, Hermes over those that are more shrewd than adventurous; and in short the nations over which the gods preside follow each the essential character of their proper god. Now if experience does not bear witness to the truth of our teachings, let us grant that our traditions are a figment and a misplaced attempt to convince, **116.** and then we ought to approve the doctrines held by you. If, however, quite the contrary is true, and from the remotest past experience bears witness to our account and in no case does anything appear to harmonise with your teachings, why do you persist in maintaining a pretension so enormous?

Come, tell me why it is that the Celts and the Germans are fierce,[36] while the Hellenes and Romans are, generally speaking, inclined to political life and humane, though at the same time unyielding and warlike? Why the Egyptians are more intelligent and more given to crafts, and the Syrians unwarlike and effeminate, but at the same time intelligent, hot-tempered, vain and quick to learn? For if there is anyone who does not discern a reason for these differences among the nations, but rather declaims that all this so befell spontaneously, how, I ask, can he still believe that the universe is administered by a providence? But if there is any man who maintains that there are reasons for these differences, let him tell me them, in the name of the creator himself, and instruct me. **131.** As for men's laws, it is evident that men have established them to correspond with their own natural dispositions; that is to say, constitutional and humane laws were established by those in whom a humane disposition had been fostered above all else, savage and inhuman laws by those in whom there lurked and was inherent the contrary disposition. For lawgivers have succeeded in adding but little by their discipline to the natural characters and aptitudes of men. Accordingly the Scythians would not receive Anacharsis[37] among them when he was inspired by a religious frenzy, and with very few exceptions you will not find that any men of the Western nations[38] have any great inclination for philosophy or geometry or studies of that sort, although the Roman Empire has now so long been paramount. But those who are unusually talented delight only in debate and the art of rhetoric, and do not adopt any other study; so strong, it seems, is the force of nature. Whence then come these differences of character and laws among the nations?

134. Now of the dissimilarity of language Moses has given a wholly fabulous explanation. For he said that the sons of men came together intending to build a city, and a great tower therein, but that God said that he must go down and confound their languages. And that no one may think I am falsely accusing him of this, I will read from the book of Moses what follows: "And they said, Go to, let us build us a city and a tower, whose top may reach unto heaven; and let us make us a name, before we be scattered abroad upon the face of the whole earth. And the Lord came down to see the city and the tower, which the children of men had builded. And the Lord said, Behold, the people is one, **135.** and they have all one language; and this they have begun to do; and now nothing will be withholden from them which they purpose to do. Go to, let us go down, and there confound their language, that no man may understand the speech of his neighbour. So the Lord God scattered them abroad upon the face of all the earth: and they left off to build the city and the tower."[39] And then you demand that we should believe this account, while you yourselves disbelieve Homer's narrative of the Aloadae, namely that they planned to set three mountains one on another, "that so the heavens might be scaled."[40] For my part I say that this tale is almost as fabulous as the other. But if you accept the former, why in the name of the gods do you discredit Homer's fable? For I suppose that to men so ignorant as you I must say nothing about the fact that, even if all men throughout the inhabited world ever employ one speech and one language, they will not be able to build a tower that will reach to the heavens, even though they should turn the whole earth into bricks. For such a tower will need countless bricks each one as large as the whole earth, if they are to succeed in reaching to the orbit of the moon. For let us assume that all mankind met together, employing but one language and speech, and that they made the whole earth into bricks and hewed out stones, when would it reach as high as the heavens, even though they spun it out and stretched it till it was finer than a thread? Then do you, who believe that this so obvious fable is true, and moreover think that God was afraid of the brutal violence of men, and for this reason came down to earth to confound their languages, do you, I say, still venture to boast of your knowledge of God?

137. But I will go back again to the question how God confounded their languages. The reason why he did so Moses has declared: namely, that God was afraid that if they should have one language and were of one mind, they would first construct for themselves a path to the heavens **138.** and then do some mischief against him. But how he carried this out Moses does not say at all, but only that he first came down from heaven, – because he could not, as it seems, do it from on high, without coming down to earth. But with respect to the existing differences in characters and customs, neither Moses nor anyone else has enlightened us. And yet among mankind the difference between the customs and the political constitutions of the nations is in every way greater than the difference in their language. What Hellene, for instance, ever tells us that a man ought to marry his sister or his daughter or his mother? Yet in Persia this is accounted virtuous. But why need I go over their several characteristics, or describe the love of liberty and lack of discipline of the Germans, the docility and tameness of the Syrians, the Persians, the Parthians, and in short of all the barbarians in the East and the South, and of all nations who possess and are contented with a somewhat despotic form of government? Now if these differences that are greater and more important came about without the aid of a greater and more divine providence, why do we vainly trouble ourselves about and worship one who takes no thought for us? For is it fitting that he who cared nothing for our lives, our characters, our manners, our good government, our political constitution, should still claim to receive honour at our hands? Certainly not. You see to what an absurdity your doctrine comes. For of all the blessings that we behold in the life of man, those that relate to the soul come first, and those that relate to the body are secondary. If, therefore, he paid no heed to our spiritual blessings, neither took thought for our physical conditions, and moreover, did not send to us teachers or lawgivers as he did for the Hebrews, such as Moses and the prophets who followed him, for what shall we properly feel gratitude to him?

141. But consider whether God has not given to us also gods[41] and kindly guardians of whom you have no knowledge, gods in no way inferior to him who from the beginning has been held in honour among the Hebrews of Judaea, the only land that he chose to take thought for, as Moses declared and those who came after him, down to our own time. But even if he who is honoured among the Hebrews really was the immediate creator of the universe, our beliefs about him are higher than theirs, and he has bestowed on us greater blessings than on them, with respect both to the soul and to externals. Of these, however, I shall speak a little later. Moreover, he sent to us also lawgivers not inferior to Moses, if indeed many of them were not far superior.

143. Therefore, as I said, unless for every nation separately some presiding national god (and under him an angel,[42] a demon, a hero, and a peculiar order of spirits which obey and work for the higher powers) established the differences in our laws and characters, you must demonstrate to me how these differences arose by some other agency. Moreover, it is not sufficient to say, "God spake and it was so." For the natures of things that are created ought to harmonise with the commands of God. I will say more clearly what I mean. Did God ordain that fire should mount upwards by chance and earth sink down? Was it not necessary, in order that the ordinance of God should be fulfilled, for the former to be light and the latter to weigh heavy? And in the case of other things also this is equally true. . . .[43] Likewise with respect to things divine. But the reason is that the race of men is doomed to death and perishable. Therefore men's works also are naturally perishable and mutable and subject to every kind of alteration. But since God is eternal, it follows that of such sort are his ordinances also. And since they are such, they are either the natures of things or are accordant with the nature of things. For how could nature be at variance with the ordinance of God? How could it fall out of harmony therewith? Therefore, if he did ordain that even as our languages are confounded and do not harmonise with one another, so too should it be with the political constitutions of the nations, then it was not by a special, isolated decree that he gave these constitutions their essential characteristics, or framed us also to match this lack of agreement.[44] For different natures must first have existed in all those things that among the nations were to be differentiated. This at any rate is seen if one observes how very different in their bodies are the Germans and Scythians from the Libyans and Ethiopians. Can this also be due to a bare decree, and does not the climate or the country have a joint influence with the gods in determining what sort of complexion they have?

146. Furthermore, Moses also consciously drew a veil over this sort of enquiry, and did not assign the confusion of dialects to God alone. For he says[45] that God did not descend alone, but that there descended with him not one but several, and he did not say who these were. But it is evident that he assumed that the beings who descended with God resembled him. If, therefore, it was not the Lord alone but his associates with him who descended for the purpose of confounding the dialects, it is very evident that for the confusion of men's characters, also, not the Lord alone but also those who together with him confounded the dialects would reasonably be considered responsible for this division.

148. Now why have I discussed this matter at such length, though it was my intention to speak briefly? For this reason: If the immediate creator of the universe be he who is proclaimed by Moses, then we hold nobler beliefs concerning him, inasmuch as we consider him to be the master of all things in general, but that there are besides national gods who are subordinate to him and are like viceroys of a king, each administering separately his own province; and, moreover, we do not make him the sectional rival of the gods whose station is subordinate to his. But if Moses first pays honour to a sectional god, and then makes the lordship of the whole universe contrast with his power, then it is better to believe as we do, and to recognise the God of the All, though not without apprehending also the God of Moses; this is better, I say, than to honour one who has been assigned the lordship over a very small portion, instead of the creator of all things.

152. That is a surprising law of Moses, I mean the famous decalogue! "Thou shalt not steal." "Thou shalt not kill." "Thou shalt not bear false witness." But let me write out word for word every one of the commandments which he says were written by God himself.

"I am the Lord thy God, which have brought thee out of the land of Egypt."[46] Then follows the second: "Thou shalt have no other gods but me." "Thou shalt not make unto thee any graven image."[47] And then he adds the reason: " For I the Lord thy God am a jealous God, visiting the iniquity of the fathers upon the children unto the third generation." "Thou shalt not take the name of the Lord thy God in vain." "Remember the sabbath day." "Honour thy father and thy mother." " Thou shalt not commit adultery." "Thou shalt not kill." "Thou shalt not steal." "Thou shalt not bear false witness." "Thou shalt not covet anything that is thy neighbour's."[48]

Now except for the command "Thou shalt not worship other gods," and "Remember the sabbath day," what nation is there, I ask in the name of the gods, which does not think that it ought to keep the other commandments? So much so that penalties have been ordained against those who transgress them, sometimes more severe, and sometimes similar to those enacted by Moses, though they are sometimes more humane.

155. But as for the commandment "Thou shalt not worship other gods," to this surely he adds a terrible libel upon God. "For I am a jealous God," he says, and in another place again, "Our God is a consuming fire."[49] Then if a man is jealous and envious you think him blameworthy, whereas if God is called jealous you think it a divine quality? And yet how is it reasonable to speak falsely of God in a matter that is so evident? For if he is indeed jealous, then against his will are all other gods worshipped, and against his will do all the remaining nations worship their gods. Then how is it that he did not himself restrain them, if he is so jealous and does not wish that the others should be worshipped, but only himself? Can it be that he was not able to do so, or did he not wish even from the beginning to prevent the other gods also from being worshipped? However, the first explanation is impious, to say, I mean, that he was unable; and the second is in accordance with what we do ourselves. Lay aside this nonsense and do not draw down on yourselves such terrible blasphemy. For if it is God's will that none other should be worshipped, why do you worship this spurious son of his whom he has never yet recognised or considered as his own? This I shall easily prove. You, however, I know not why, foist on him a counterfeit son. . . .[50]

160. Nowhere[51] is God shown as angry, or resentful, or wroth, or taking an oath, or inclining first to this side, then suddenly to that, or as turned from his purpose, as Moses tells us happened in the case of Phinehas. If any of you has read the Book of Numbers he knows what I mean. For when Phinehas had seized with his own hand and slain the man who had dedicated himself to Baal-peor, and with him the woman who had persuaded him, striking her with a shameful and most painful wound through the belly, as Moses tells us, then God is made to say: "Phinehas, the son of Eleazar, the son of Aaron the priest, hath turned my wrath away from the children of Israel, in that he was jealous with my jealousy among them; and I consumed not the children of Israel in my jealousy."[52] What could be more trivial than the reason for which God was falsely represented as angry by the writer of this passage? **161.** What could be more irrational, even if ten or fifteen persons, or even, let us suppose, a hundred, for they certainly will not say that there were a thousand, – however, let us assume that even as many persons as that ventured to transgress some one of the laws laid down by God; was it right that on account of this one thousand, six hundred thousand should be utterly destroyed? For my part I think it would be better in every way to preserve one bad man along with a thousand virtuous men than to destroy the thousand together with that one. . . .[53]

For if the anger of even one hero or unimportant demon is hard to bear for whole countries and cities, who could have endured the wrath of so mighty a God, whether it were directed against demons or angels or mankind? **168.** It is worth while to compare his behaviour with the mildness of Lycurgus and the forbearance of Solon, or the kindness and benevolence of the Romans towards transgressors. **171.** But observe also from what follows how far superior are our teachings to theirs. The philosophers bid us imitate the gods so far as we can, and they teach us that this imitation consists in the contemplation of realities. And that this sort of study is remote from passion and is indeed based on freedom from passion, is, I suppose, evident, even without my saying it. In proportion then as we, having been assigned to the contemplation of realities, attain to freedom from passion, in so far do we become like God. But what sort of imitation of God is praised among the Hebrews? Anger and wrath and fierce jealousy. For God says: "Phinehas hath turned away my wrath from the children of Israel, in that he was jealous with my jealousy among them." For God, on finding one who shared his resentment and his grief, thereupon, as it appears, laid aside his resentment. **172.** These words and others like them about God Moses is frequently made to utter in the Scripture.

176. Furthermore observe from what follows that God did not take thought for the Hebrews alone, but though he cared for all nations, he bestowed on the Hebrews nothing considerable or of great value, whereas on us he bestowed gifts far higher and surpassing theirs. For instance the Egyptians, as they reckon up the names of not a few wise men among themselves, can boast that they possess many successors of Hermes, I mean of Hermes who in his third manifestation visited Egypt;[54] while the Chaldaeans and Assyrians can boast of the successors of Oannes[55] and Belos;[56] the Hellenes can boast of countless successors of Cheiron.[57] For thenceforth all Hellenes were born with an aptitude for the mysteries and theologians, in the very way, you observe, which the Hebrews claim as their own peculiar boast. . . .[58]

178. But has God granted to you to originate any science or any philosophical study? Why, what is it? For the theory of the heavenly bodies was perfected among the Hellenes, after the first observations had been made among the barbarians in Babylon.[59] And the study of geometry took its rise in the measurement of the land in Egypt, and from this grew to its present importance. Arithmetic began with the Phoenician merchants, and among the Hellenes in course of time acquired the aspect of a regular science. These three the Hellenes combined with music into one science, for they connected astronomy with geometry and adapted arithmetic to both, and perceived the principle of harmony in it. Hence they laid down the rules for their music, since they had discovered for the laws of harmony with reference to the sense of hearing an agreement that was infallible, or something very near to it.[60]

184. Need I tell over their names man by man, or under their professions? I mean, either the individual men, as for instance Plato, Socrates, Aristeides, Cimon, Thales, Lycurgus, Agesilaus, Archidamus, – or should I rather speak of the class of philosophers, of generals, of artificers, of lawgivers? For it will be found that even the most wicked and most brutal of the generals behaved more mildly to the greatest offenders than Moses did to those who had done no wrong. And now of what monarchy shall I report to you? **190.** Shall it be that of Perseus, or Aeacus, or Minos of Crete, who purified the sea of pirates, and expelled and drove out the barbarians as far as Syria and Sicily, advancing in both directions the frontiers of his realm, and ruled not only over the islands but also over the dwellers along the coasts? And dividing with his brother Rhadamanthus, not indeed the earth, but the care of mankind, he himself laid down the laws as he received them from Zeus, but left to Rhadamanthus to fill the part of judge. . . .[61]

193. But when after her[62] foundation many wars encompassed her, she won and prevailed in them all; and since she ever increased in size in proportion to her very dangers and needed greater security, then Zeus set over her the great philosopher Numa.[63] This then was the excellent and upright Numa who dwelt in deserted groves and ever communed with the gods in the pure thoughts of his own heart. . . .[64] It was he who established most of the laws concerning temple worship. **194.** Now these blessings, derived from a divine possession and inspiration which proceeded both from the Sibyl and others who at that time uttered oracles in their native tongue, were manifestly bestowed on the city by Zeus. And the shield which fell from the clouds[65] and the head which appeared on the hill,[66] from which, I suppose, the seat of mighty Zeus received its name, are we to reckon these among the very highest or among secondary gifts? And yet, ye misguided men, though there is preserved among us that weapon which flew down from heaven, which mighty Zeus or father Ares sent down to give us a warrant, not in word but in deed, that he will forever hold his shield before our city, you have ceased to adore and reverence it, but you adore the wood of the cross and draw its likeness on your foreheads and engrave it on your housefronts.

Would not any man be justified in detesting the more intelligent among you, or pitying the more foolish, who, by following you, have sunk to such depths of ruin that they have abandoned the ever-living gods and have gone over to the corpse of the Jew.[67] . . . **197.** For I say nothing about the Mysteries of the Mother of the Gods, and I admire Marius. . . . **198.** For the spirit that comes to men from the gods is present but seldom and in few, and it is not easy for every man to share in it or at every time. Thus it is that the prophetic spirit has ceased among the Hebrews also, nor is it maintained among the Egyptians, either, down to the present. And we see that the indigenous oracles[68] of Greece have also fallen silent and yielded to the course of time. Then lo, our gracious lord and father Zeus took thought of this, and that we might not be wholly deprived of communion with the gods has granted us through the sacred arts[69] a means of enquiry by which we may obtain the aid that suffices for our needs.

200. I had almost forgotten the greatest of the gifts of Helios and Zeus. But naturally I kept it for the last. And indeed it is not peculiar to us Romans only, but we share it, I think, with the Hellenes our kinsmen. I mean to say that Zeus engendered Asclepius from himself among the intelligible gods,[70] and through the life of generative Helios he revealed him to the earth. Asclepius, having made his visitation to earth from the sky, appeared at Epidaurus singly, in the shape of a man; but afterwards he multiplied himself, and by his visitations stretched out over the whole earth his saving right hand. He came to Pergamon, to Ionia, to Tarentum afterwards; and later he came to Rome. And he travelled to Cos and thence to Aegae. Next he is present everywhere on land and sea. He visits no one of us separately, and yet he raises up souls that are sinful and bodies that are sick.

201. But what great gift of this sort do the Hebrews boast of as bestowed on them by God, the Hebrews who have persuaded you to desert to them? If you had at any rate paid heed to their teachings, you would not have fared altogether ill, and though worse than you did before, when you were with us, still your condition would have been bearable and supportable. For you would be worshipping one god instead of many, not a man, or rather many wretched men.[71] **202.** And though you would be following a law that is harsh and stern and contains much that is savage and barbarous, instead of our mild and humane laws, and would in other respects be inferior to us, yet you would be more holy and purer than now in your forms of worship. But now it has come to pass that like leeches you have sucked the worst blood from that source and left the purer. **191.** Yet Jesus, who won over the least worthy of you, has been known by name for but little more than three hundred years: and during his lifetime he accomplished nothing worth hearing of, unless anyone thinks that to heal crooked and blind men and to exorcise those who were possessed by evil demons in the villages of Bethsaida and Bethany can be classed as a mighty achievement. **205.** As for purity of life you do not know whether he so much as mentioned it; but you emulate the rages and the bitterness of the Jews, overturning temples and altars,[72] **206.** and you slaughtered not only those of us who remained true to the teachings of their fathers, but also men who were as much astray as yourselves, heretics,[73] because they did not wail over the corpse[74] in the same fashion as yourselves. But these are rather your own doings; for nowhere did either Jesus or Paul hand down to you such commands. The reason for this is that they never even hoped that you would one day attain to such power as you have; for they were content if they could delude maidservants and slaves, and through them the women, and men like Cornelius[75] and Sergius.[76] But if you can show me that one of these men is mentioned by the well-known writers of that time, – these events happened in the reign of Tiberius or Claudius, – then you may consider that I speak falsely about all matters.

209. But I know not whence I was as it were inspired to utter these remarks. However, to return to the point at which I digressed,[77] when I asked, "Why were you so ungrateful to our gods as to desert them for the Jews?" Was it because the gods granted the sovereign power to Rome, permitting the Jews to be free for a short time only, and then forever to be enslaved and aliens? Look at Abraham: was he not an alien in a strange land? And Jacob: was he not a slave, first in Syria, then after that in Palestine, and in his old age in Egypt? Does not Moses say that he led them forth from the house of bondage out of Egypt "with a stretched out arm"?[78] And after their sojourn in Palestine did they not change their fortunes more frequently than observers say the chameleon changes its colour, now subject to the judges,[79] now enslaved to foreign races? And when they began to be governed by kings, – but let me for the present postpone asking how they were governed: for as the Scripture tells us,[80] God did not willingly allow them to have kings, but only when constrained by them, **210.** and after protesting to them beforehand that they would thus be governed ill, – still they did at any rate inhabit their own country and tilled it for a little over three hundred years. After that they were enslaved first to the Assyrians, then to the Medes, later to the Persians, and now at last to ourselves. **213.** Even Jesus, who was proclaimed among you, was one of Caesar's subjects. And if you do not believe me I will prove it a little later, or rather let me simply assert it now. However, you admit that with his father and mother he registered his name in the governorship of Cyrenius.[81]

But when he became man what benefits did he confer on his own kinsfolk? Nay, the Galilaeans answer, they refused to hearken unto Jesus. What? How was it then that this hardhearted[82] and stubborn-necked people hearkened unto Moses; but Jesus, who commanded the spirits[83] and walked on the sea, and drove out demons, and as you yourselves assert made the heavens and the earth, – for no one of his disciples ventured to say this concerning him, save only John, and he did not say it clearly or distinctly; still let us at any rate admit that he said it – could not this Jesus change the dispositions of his own friends and kinsfolk to the end that he might save them?

218. However, I will consider this again a little later when I begin to examine particularly into the miracle-working and the fabrication of the gospels. But now answer me this. Is it better to be free continuously and during two thousand whole years to rule over the greater part of the earth and the sea, or to be enslaved and to live in obedience to the will of others? No man is so lacking in self-respect as to choose the latter by preference. Again, will anyone think that victory in war is less desirable than defeat? Who is so stupid? But if this that I assert is the truth, point out to me among the Hebrews a single general like Alexander or Caesar! You have no such man. And indeed, by the gods, I am well aware that I am insulting these heroes by the question, but I mentioned them because they are well known. For the generals who are inferior to them are unknown to the multitude, and yet every one of them deserves more admiration than all the generals put together whom the Jews have had.

221. Further, as regards the constitution of the state and the fashion of the law-courts, the administration of cities and the excellence of the laws, progress in learning and the cultivation of the liberal arts, were not all these things in a miserable and barbarous state among the Hebrews? **222.** And yet the wretched Eusebius[84] will have it that poems in hexameters are to be found even among them, and sets up a claim that the study of logic exists among the Hebrews, since he has heard among the Hellenes the word they use for logic. What kind of healing art has ever appeared among the Hebrews, like that of Hippocrates among the Hellenes, and of certain other schools that came after him? **224.** Is their "wisest" man Solomon at all comparable with Phocylides or Theognis or Isocrates among the Hellenes? Certainly not. At least, if one were to compare the exhortations of Isocrates with Solomon's proverbs, you would, I am very sure, find that the son of Theodoras is superior to their "wisest" king. "But," they answer, "Solomon was also proficient in the secret cult of God." What then? Did not this Solomon serve our gods also, deluded by his wife, as they assert?[85] What great virtue! What wealth of wisdom! He could not rise superior to pleasure, and the arguments of a woman led him astray! Then if he was deluded by a woman, do not call this man wise. But if you are convinced that he was wise, do not believe that he was deluded by a woman, but that, trusting to his own judgement and intelligence and the teaching that he received from the God who had been revealed to him, he served the other gods also. For envy and jealousy do not come even near the most virtuous men, much more are they remote from angels and gods. But you concern yourselves with incomplete and partial powers,[86] which if anyone call daemonic he does not err. For in them are pride and vanity, but in the gods there is nothing of the sort.

229. If the reading of your own scriptures is sufficient for you, why do you nibble at the learning of the Hellenes? And yet it were better to keep men away from that learning than from the eating of sacrificial meat. For by that, as even Paul says,[87] he who eats thereof is not harmed, but the conscience of the brother who sees him might be offended according to you, O most wise and arrogant men! But this learning of ours has caused every noble being that nature has produced among you to abandon impiety. Accordingly everyone who possessed even a small fraction of innate virtue has speedily abandoned your impiety. It were therefore better for you to keep men from learning rather than from sacrificial meats. But you yourselves know, it seems to me, the very different effect on the intelligence of your writings as compared with ours; and that from studying yours no man could attain to excellence or even to ordinary goodness, whereas from studying ours every man would become better than before, even though he were altogether without natural fitness. But when a man is naturally well endowed, and moreover receives the education of our literature, he becomes actually a gift of the gods to mankind, either by kindling the light of knowledge, or by founding some kind of political constitution, or by routing numbers of his country's foes, or even by travelling far over the earth and far by sea, and thus proving himself a man of heroic mould. . .[88]

Now this would be a clear proof: Choose out children from among you all and train and educate them in your scriptures, **230.** and if when they come to manhood they prove to have nobler qualities than slaves, then you may believe that I am talking nonsense and am suffering from spleen. Yet you are so misguided and foolish that you regard those chronicles of yours as divinely inspired, though by their help no man could ever become wiser or braver or better than he was before; while, on the other hand, writings by whose aid men can acquire courage, wisdom and justice, these you ascribe to Satan and to those who serve Satan!

235. Asclepius heals our bodies, and the Muses with the aid of Asclepius and Apollo and Hermes, the god of eloquence, train our souls; Ares fights for us in war and Enyo also; Hephaistus apportions and administers the crafts, and Athene the Motherless Maiden with the aid of Zeus presides over them all. Consider therefore whether we are not superior to you in every single one of these things, I mean in the arts and in wisdom and intelligence; and this is true, whether you consider the useful arts or the imitative arts whose end is beauty, such as the statuary's art, painting, or household management, and the art of healing derived from Asclepius whose oracles are found everywhere on earth, and the god grants to us a share in them perpetually. At any rate, when I have been sick, Asclepius has often cured me by prescribing remedies; and of this Zeus is witness. Therefore, if we who have not given ourselves over to the spirit of apostasy, fare better than you in soul and body and external affairs, why do you abandon these teachings of ours and go over to those others?

238. And why is it that you do not abide even by the traditions of the Hebrews or accept the law which God has given to them? Nay, you have forsaken their teaching even more than ours, abandoning the religion of your forefathers and giving yourselves over to the predictions of the prophets? For if any man should wish to examine into the truth concerning you, he will find that your impiety is compounded of the rashness of the Jews and the indifference and vulgarity of the Gentiles.[89] For from both sides you have drawn what is by no means their best but their inferior teaching, and so have made for yourselves a border[90] of wickedness. For the Hebrews have precise laws concerning religious worship, and countless sacred things and observances which demand the priestly life and profession. But though their lawgiver forbade them to serve all the gods save only that one, whose "portion is Jacob, and Israel an allotment of his inheritance ";[91] though he did not say this only, but methinks added also "Thou shalt not revile the gods";[92] yet the shamelessness and audacity of later generations, desiring to root out all reverence from the mass of the people, has thought that blasphemy accompanies the neglect of worship. This, in fact, is the only thing that you have drawn from this source; for in all other respects you and the Jews have nothing in common. Nay, it is from the new-fangled teaching of the Hebrews that you have seized upon this blasphemy of the gods who are honoured among us; but the reverence for every higher nature, characteristic of our religious worship, combined with the love of the traditions of our forefathers, you have cast off, and have acquired only the habit of eating all things, "even as the green herb."[93] But to tell the truth, you have taken pride in outdoing our vulgarity, (this, I think, is a thing that happens to all nations, and very naturally) and you thought that you must adapt your ways to the lives of the baser sort, shopkeepers,[94] tax-gatherers, dancers and libertines.

245. But that not only the Galilaeans of our day but also those of the earliest time, those who were the first to receive the teaching from Paul, were men of this sort, is evident from the testimony of Paul himself in a letter addressed to them. For unless he actually knew that they had committed all these disgraceful acts, he was not, I think, so impudent as to write to those men themselves concerning their conduct, in language for which, even though in the same letter he included as many eulogies of them, he ought to have blushed, yes, even if those eulogies were deserved, while if they were false and fabricated, then he ought to have sunk into the ground to escape seeming to behave with wanton flattery and slavish adulation. But the following are the very words that Paul wrote concerning those who had heard his teaching, and were addressed to the men themselves: "Be not deceived: neither idolaters, nor adulterers, nor effeminate, nor abusers of themselves with men, nor thieves, nor covetous, nor drunkards, nor revilers, nor extortioners, shall inherit the kingdom of God. And of this ye are not ignorant, brethren, that such were you also; but ye washed yourselves, but ye were sanctified in the name of Jesus Christ."[95] Do you see that he says that these men too had been of such sort, but that they "had been sanctified" and "had been washed," water being able to cleanse and winning power to purify when it shall go down into the soul? And baptism does not take away his leprosy from the leper, or scabs, or pimples, or warts, or gout, or dysentery, or dropsy, or a whitlow, in fact no disorder of the body, great or small, then shall it do away with adultery and theft and in short all the transgressions of the soul? . . .[96]

253. Now since the Galilaeans say that, though they are different from the Jews, they are still, precisely speaking, Israelites in accordance with their prophets, and that they obey Moses above all and the prophets who in Judaea succeeded him, let us see in what respect they chiefly agree with those prophets. And let us begin with the teaching of Moses, who himself also, as they claim, foretold the birth of Jesus that was to be. Moses, then, not once or twice or thrice but very many times says that men ought to honour one God only, and in fact names him the Highest; but that they ought to honour any other god he nowhere says. He speaks of angels and lords and moreover of several gods, but from these he chooses out the first and does not assume any god as second, either like or unlike him, such as you have invented. And if among you perchance you possess a single utterance of Moses with respect to this, you are bound to produce it. For the words "A prophet shall the Lord your God raise up unto you of your brethren, like unto me; to him shall ye hearken,"[97] were certainly not said of the son of Mary. And even though, to please you, one should concede that they were said of him, Moses says that the prophet will be like him and not like God, a prophet like himself and born of men, not of a god. And the words " The sceptre shall not depart from Judah, nor a leader from his loins,"[98] were most certainly not said of the son of Mary, but of the royal house of David, which, you observe, came to an end with King Zedekiah. And certainly the Scripture can be interpreted in two ways when it says "until there comes what is reserved for him "; but you have wrongly interpreted it "until he comes for whom it is reserved."[99] But it is very clear that not one of these sayings relates to Jesus; for he is not even from Judah. How could he be when according to you he was not born of Joseph but of the Holy Spirit? For though in your genealogies you trace Joseph back to Judah, you could not invent even this plausibly. For Matthew and Luke are refuted by the fact that they disagree concerning his genealogy.[100] **261.** However, as I intend to examine closely into the truth of this matter in my Second Book, I leave it till then.[101] But granted that he really is "a sceptre from Judah," then he is not "God born of God," as you are in the habit of saying, nor is it true that "All things were made by him; and without him was not any thing made."[102] But, say you, we are told in the Book of Numbers also: "There shall arise a star out of Jacob, and a man out of Israel."[103] It is certainly clear that this relates to David and to his descendants; for David was a son of Jesse.

If therefore you try to prove anything from these writings, show me a single saying that you have drawn from that source whence I have drawn very many. But that Moses believed in one God, the God of Israel, he says in *Deuteronomy*: "So that thou mightest know that the Lord thy God he is one God; and there is none else beside him."[104] **262.** And moreover he says besides, "And lay it to thine heart that this the Lord thy God is God in the heaven above and upon the earth beneath, and there is none else."[105] And again, "Hear, O Israel: the Lord our God is one Lord."[106] And again, "See that I am and there is no God save me."[107] These then are the words of Moses when he insists that there is only one God. But perhaps the Galilaeans will reply: "But we do not assert that there are two gods or three." But I will show that they do assert this also, and I call John to witness, who says: "In the beginning was the Word, and the Word was with God and the Word was God."[108] You see that the Word is said to be with God? Now whether this is he who was born of Mary or someone else, – that I may answer Photinus[109] at the same time, – this now makes no difference; indeed I leave the dispute to you; but it is enough to bring forward the evidence that he says "with God," and "in the beginning." How then does this agree with the teachings of Moses?

"But," say the Galilaeans, "it agrees with the teachings of Isaiah. For Isaiah says, 'Behold the virgin shall conceive and bear a son.' "[110] Now granted that this is said about a god, though it is by no means so stated; for a married woman who before her conception had lain with her husband was no virgin, – but let us admit that it is said about her, – does Isaiah anywhere say that a god will be born of the virgin? But why do you not cease to call Mary the mother of God, if Isaiah nowhere says that he that is born of the virgin is the "only begotten Son of God"[111] and "the firstborn of all creation"?[112] But as for the saying of John, "All things were made by him; and without him was not any thing made that was made,"[113] can anyone point this out among the utterances of the prophets? But now listen to the sayings that I point out to you from those same prophets, one after another. "O Lord our God, make us thine; we know none other beside thee."[114] And Hezekiah the king has been represented by them as praying as follows: "O Lord God of Israel, that sittest upon the Cherubim, thou art God, even thou alone."[115] Does he leave any place for the second god? **276.** But if, as you believe, the Word is God born of God and proceeded from the substance of the Father, why do you say that the virgin is the mother of God? For how could she bear a god since she is, according to you, a human being? And moreover, when God declares plainly "I am he, and there is none that can deliver beside me,"[116] **277.** do you dare to call her son Saviour?

290. And that Moses calls the angels gods you may hear from his own words, "The sons of God saw the daughters of men that they were fair; and they took them wives of all which they chose."[117] And a little further on: "And also after that, when the sons of God came in unto the daughters of men, and they bare children to them, the same became the giants which were of old, the men of renown."[118] Now that he means the angels is evident, and this has not been foisted on him from without, but it is clear also from his saying that not men but giants were born from them. For it is clear that if he had thought that men and not beings of some higher and more powerful nature were their fathers, he would not have said that the giants were their offspring. For it seems to me that he declared that the race of giants arose from the mixture of mortal and immortal. Again, when Moses speaks of many sons of God and calls them not men but angels, would he not then have revealed to mankind, if he had known thereof, God the "only begotten Word," or a son of God or however you call him? But is it because he did not think this of great importance that he says concerning Israel, "Israel is my firstborn son?"[119] Why did not Moses say this about Jesus also? He taught that there was only one God, but that he had many sons who divided the nations among themselves. But the Word as firstborn son of God or as a God, or any of those fictions which have been invented by you later, he neither knew at all nor taught openly thereof. You have now heard Moses himself and the other prophets. **291.** Moses, therefore, utters many sayings to the following effect and in many places: "Thou shalt fear the Lord thy God and him only shalt thou serve."[120] How then has it been handed down in the Gospels that Jesus commanded: "Go ye therefore and teach all nations, baptising them in the name of the Father, and of the Son, and of the Holy Ghost,"[121] if they were not intended to serve him also? And your beliefs also are in harmony with these commands, when along with the Father you pay divine honours to the son. . . [122]

And now observe again how much Moses says about the deities that avert evil: "And he shall take two he-goats of the goats for a sin-offering, and one ram for a burnt offering. **299.** And Aaron shall bring also his bullock of the sin-offering, which is for himself, and make an atonement for himself and for his house. And he shall take the two goats and present them before the Lord at the door of the tabernacle of the covenant. And Aaron shall cast lots upon the two goats; one lot for the Lord and the other lot for the scape-goat"[123] so as to send him forth, says Moses, as a scape-goat, and let him loose into the wilderness. Thus then is sent forth the goat that is sent for a scape-goat. And of the second goat Moses says: "Then shall he kill the goat of the sin-offering that is for the people before the Lord, and bring his blood within the vail, and shall sprinkle the blood upon the altar-step,[124] and shall make an atonement for the holy place, because of the uncleanness of the children of Israel and because of their transgressions in all their sins."[125] **305.** Accordingly it is evident from what has been said, that Moses knew the various methods of sacrifice. And to show that he did not think them impure as you do, listen again to his own words. "But the soul that eateth of the flesh of the sacrifice of peace-offerings that pertain unto the Lord, having his uncleanness upon him, even that soul shall be cut off from his people."[126] So cautious is Moses himself with regard to the eating of the flesh of sacrifice.

But now I had better remind you of what I said earlier,[127] since on account of that I have said this also. Why is it, I repeat, that after deserting us you do not accept the law of the Jews or abide by the sayings of Moses? No doubt some sharp-sighted person will answer, "The Jews too do not sacrifice." But I will convict him of being terribly dull-sighted, for in the first place I reply that neither do you also observe any one of the other customs observed by the Jews; and, secondly, that the Jews do sacrifice in their own houses, **306.** and even to this day everything that they eat is consecrated; and they pray before sacrificing, and give the right shoulder to the priests as the firstfruits; but since they have been deprived of their temple, or, as they are accustomed to call it, their holy place, they are prevented from offering the firstfruits of the sacrifice to God.[128] But why do you not sacrifice, since you have invented your new kind of sacrifice and do not need Jerusalem at all? And yet it was superfluous to ask you this question, since I said the same thing at the beginning, when I wished to show that the Jews agree with the Gentiles, except that they believe in only one God. That is indeed peculiar to them and strange to us; since all the rest we have in a manner in common with them – temples, sanctuaries, altars, purifications, and certain precepts. For as to these we differ from one another either not at all or in trivial matters. . . .[129]

314. Why in your diet are you not as pure as the Jews, and why do you say that we ought to eat everything "even as the green herb,"[130] putting your faith in Peter, because, as the Galilaeans say, he declared, "What God hath cleansed, that make not thou common"?[131] What proof is there of this, that of old God held certain things abominable, but now has made them pure? For Moses, when he is laying down the law concerning four-footed things, says that whatsoever parteth the hoof and is cloven-footed and cheweth the cud[132] is pure, but that which is not of this sort is impure. Now if, after the vision of Peter, the pig has now taken to chewing the cud, then let us obey Peter; for it is in very truth a miracle if, after the vision of Peter, it has taken to that habit. But if he spoke falsely when he said that he saw this revelation, – to use your own way of speaking, – in the house of the tanner, why are we so ready to believe him in such important matters? Was it so hard a thing that Moses enjoined on you when, besides the flesh of swine, he forbade you to eat winged things and things that dwell in the sea, and declared to you that besides the flesh of swine these also had been cast out by God and shown to be impure?

319. But why do I discuss at length these teachings of theirs,[133] when we may easily see whether they have any force? For they assert that God, after the earlier law, appointed the second. For, say they, the former arose with a view to a certain occasion and was circumscribed by definite periods of time, but this later law was revealed because the law of Moses was circumscribed by time and place. That they say this falsely I will clearly show by quoting from the books of Moses not merely ten but ten thousand passages as evidence, where he says that the law is for all time. Now listen to a passage from *Exodus*: "And this day shall be unto you for a memorial; and ye shall keep it a feast to the Lord throughout your generations; ye shall keep it a feast by an ordinance forever; the first day shall ye put away leaven out of your houses." . . .[134] Many passages to the same effect are still left, but on account of their number I refrain from citing them to prove that the law of Moses was to last for all time. But do you point out to me where there is any statement by Moses of what was later on rashly uttered by Paul, I mean that "Christ is the end of the law."[135] Where does God announce to the Hebrews a second law besides that which was established? **320.** Nowhere does it occur, not even a revision of the established law.[136] For listen again to the words of Moses: "Ye shall not add unto the word which I command you, neither shall ye diminish aught from it. Keep the commandments of the Lord your God which I command you this day."[137] And "Cursed be every man who does not abide by them all."[138] But you have thought it a slight thing to diminish and to add to the things which were written in the law; and to transgress it completely you have thought to be in every way more manly and more high-spirited, because you do not look to the truth but to that which will persuade all men.[139]

327. But you are so misguided that you have not even remained faithful to the teachings that were handed down to you by the apostles. And these also have been altered., so as to be worse and more impious, by those who came after. At any rate neither Paul nor Matthew nor Luke nor Mark ventured to call Jesus God. But the worthy John, since he perceived that a great number of people in many of the towns of Greece and Italy had already been infected by this disease,[140] and because he heard, I suppose, that even the tombs of Peter and Paul were being worshipped – secretly, it is true, but still he did hear this, – he, I say, was the first to venture to call Jesus God. And after he had spoken briefly about John the Baptist he referred again to the Word which he was proclaiming, and said, "And the Word was made flesh, and dwelt among us."[141] But how, he does not say, because he was ashamed. Nowhere, however, does he call him either Jesus or Christ, so long as he calls him God and the Word, but as it were insensibly and secretly he steals away our ears, and says that John the Baptist bore this witness on behalf of Jesus Christ, that in very truth he it is whom we must believe to be God the Word. **333.** But that John says this concerning Jesus Christ I for my part do not deny. And yet certain of the impious think that Jesus Christ is quite distinct from the Word that was proclaimed by John. That however is not the case. For he whom John himself calls God the Word, this is he who, says he, was recognised by John the Baptist to be Jesus Christ. Observe accordingly how cautiously, how quietly and insensibly he introduces into the drama the crowning word of his impiety; and he is so rascally and deceitful that he rears his head once more to add, "No man hath seen God at any time; the only begotten Son which is in the bosom of the Father, he hath declared him."[142] Then is this only begotten Son which is in the bosom of the Father the God who is the Word and became flesh? And if, as I think, it is indeed he, you also have certainly beheld God. For "He dwelt among you, and ye beheld his glory."[143] Why then do you add to this that "No man hath seen God at any time"? For ye have indeed seen, if not God the Father, still God who is the Word.[144] But if the only begotten Son is one person and the God who is the Word another, as I have heard from certain of your sect, then it appears that not even John made that rash statement.[145]

335. However this evil doctrine did originate with John; but who could detest as they deserve all those doctrines that you have invented as a sequel, while you keep adding many corpses newly dead to the corpse of long ago?[146] You have filled the whole world with tombs and sepulchres, and yet in your scriptures it is nowhere said that you must grovel among tombs[147] and pay them honour. But you have gone so far in iniquity that you think you need not listen even to the words of Jesus of Nazareth on this matter. Listen then to what he says about sepulchres: "Woe unto you, scribes and Pharisees, hypocrites! for ye are like unto whited sepulchres; outward the tomb appears beautiful, but within it is full of dead men's bones, and of all uncleanness."[148] If, then, Jesus said that sepulchres are full of uncleanness, how can you invoke God at them? . . .[149]

339. Therefore, since this is so, why do you grovel among tombs? Do you wish to hear the reason? It is not I who will tell you, but the prophet Isaiah: "They lodge among tombs and in caves for the sake of dream visions."[150] **340.** You observe, then, how ancient among the Jews was this work of witchcraft, namely, sleeping among tombs for the sake of dream visions. And indeed it is likely that your apostles, after their teacher's death, practised this and handed it down to you from the beginning, I mean to those who first adopted your faith, and that they themselves performed their spells more skilfully than you do, and displayed openly to those who came after them the places in which they performed this witchcraft and abomination.

343. But you, though you practise that which God from the first abhorred, as he showed through Moses and the prophets, have refused nevertheless to offer victims at the altar, and to sacrifice. "Yes," say the Galilaeans, "because fire will not descend to consume the sacrifices as in the case of Moses." Only once, I answer, did this happen in the case of Moses;[151] and again after many years in the case of Elijah the Tishbite.[152] For I will prove in a few words that Moses himself thought that it was necessary to bring fire from outside for the sacrifice, and even before him, Abraham the patriarch as well. . .[153]

346. And this is not the only instance, but when the sons of Adam also offered firstfruits to God, **347.** the Scripture says, "And the Lord had respect unto Abel and to his offerings; but unto Cain and to his offerings he had not respect. And Cain was very wroth, and his countenance fell. And the Lord God said unto Cain, Why art thou wroth? and why is thy countenance fallen? Is it not so – if thou offerest rightly, but dost not cut in pieces rightly, thou hast sinned?"[154] Do you then desire to hear also what were their offerings? "And at the end of days it came to pass that Cain brought of the fruits of the ground an offering unto the Lord. And Abel, he also brought of the firstlings of his flock and of the fat thereof."[155] You see, say the Galilaeans, it was not the sacrifice but the division thereof that God disapproved when he said to Cain, "If thou offerest rightly, but dost not cut in pieces rightly, hast thou not sinned?" This is what one of your most learned bishops[156] told me. But in the first place he was deceiving himself and then other men also. For when I asked him in what way the division was blameworthy he did not know how to get out of it, or how to make me even a frigid explanation. And when I saw that he was greatly embarrassed, I said; "God rightly disapproved the thing you speak of. For the zeal of the two men was equal, in that they both thought that they ought to offer up gifts and sacrifices to God. But in the matter of their division one of them hit the mark and the other fell short of it. How, and in what manner? Why, since of things on the earth some have life and others are lifeless, and those that have life are more precious than those that are lifeless to the living God who is also the cause of life, inasmuch as they also have a share of life and have a soul more akin to his – for this reason God was more graciously inclined to him who offered a perfect sacrifice."

351. Now I must take up this other point and ask them, Why, pray, do you not practise circumcision? "Paul," they answer, "said that circumcision of the heart but not of the flesh was granted unto Abraham because he believed.[157] Nay it was not now of the flesh that he spoke, and we ought to believe the pious words that were proclaimed by him and by Peter." On the other hand hear again that God is said to have given circumcision of the flesh to Abraham for a covenant and a sign: "This is my covenant which ye shall keep, between me and thee and thy seed after thee in their generations. Ye shall circumcise the flesh of your foreskin, and it shall be in token of a covenant betwixt me and thee and betwixt me and thy seed." . . .[158] Therefore when He[159] has undoubtedly taught that it is proper to observe the law, and threatened with punishment those who transgress one commandment, what manner of defending yourselves will you devise, you who have transgressed them all without exception? For either Jesus will be found to speak falsely, or rather you will be found in all respects and in every way to have failed to preserve the law. **354.** "The circumcision shall be of thy flesh," says Moses.[160] But the Galilaeans do not heed him, and they say: "We circumcise our hearts." By all means. For there is among you no evildoer, no sinner; so thoroughly do you circumcise your hearts.[161] They say: "We cannot observe the rule of unleavened bread or keep the Passover; for on our behalf Christ was sacrificed once and for all." Very well! Then did he forbid you to eat unleavened bread? And yet, I call the gods to witness, I am one of those who avoid keeping their festivals with the Jews; but nevertheless I revere always the God of Abraham, Isaac and Jacob;[162] who being themselves Chaldaeans, of a sacred race, skilled in theurgy, had learned the practice of circumcision while they sojourned as strangers with the Egyptians. And they revered a God who was ever gracious to me and to those who worshipped him as Abraham did, for he is a very great and powerful God, but he has nothing to do with you. For you do not imitate Abraham by erecting altars to him, or building altars of sacrifice and worshipping him as Abraham did, with sacrificial offerings. **356.** For Abraham used to sacrifice even as we Hellenes do, always and continually. And he used the method of divination from shooting stars. Probably this also is an Hellenic custom. But for higher things he augured from the flight of birds.

And he possessed also a steward of his house who set signs for himself.[163] And if one of you doubts this, the very words which were uttered by Moses concerning it will show him clearly: "After these sayings the word of the Lord came unto Abraham in a vision of the night, sayings Fear not, Abraham: I am thy shield. Thy reward shall be exceeding great. And Abraham said. Lord God what wilt thou give me? For I go childless, and the son of Masek the slave woman will be my heir. And straightway the word of the Lord came unto him saying, This man shall not be thine heir: but he that shall come forth from thee shall be thine heir. And he brought him forth and said unto him, Look now toward heaven, and tell the stars, if thou be able to number them: and he said unto him, So shall thy seed be. And Abraham believed in the Lord: and it was counted to him for righteousness."[164]

Tell me now why he who dealt with him, whether angel or God, brought him forth and showed him the stars? For while still within the house did he not know how great **357.** is the multitude of the stars that at night are always visible and shining? But I think it was because he wished to show him the shooting stars, so that as a visible pledge of his words he might offer to Abraham the decision of the heavens that fulfills and sanctions all things. **358.** And lest any man should think that such an interpretation is forced, I will convince him by adding what comes next to the above passage. For it is written next: "And he said unto him, I am the Lord that brought thee out of the land of the Chaldees, to give thee this land to inherit it. And he said, Lord God, whereby shall I know that I shall inherit it? And he said unto him, Take me an heifer of three years old, and a she-goat of three years old, and a ram of three years old, and a turtle-dove and a pigeon. And he took unto him all these, and divided them in the midst, and laid each piece one against another; but the birds divided he not. And the fowls came down upon the divided carcases, and Abraham sat down among them."

You see how the announcement of the angel or god who had appeared was strengthened by means of the augury from birds, and how the prophecy was completed, not at haphazard as happens with you, but with the accompaniment of sacrifices? Moreover he says that by the flocking together of the birds he showed that his message was true. And Abraham accepted the pledge, and moreover declared that a pledge that lacked truth seemed to be mere folly and imbecility. But it is not possible to behold the truth from speech alone, but some clear sign must follow on what has been said, a sign that by its appearance shall guarantee the prophecy that has been made concerning the future. . . . [165]

351. However, for your indolence in this matter there remains for you one single excuse, namely, that you are not permitted to sacrifice if you are outside Jerusalem, **324.** though for that matter Elijah sacrificed on Mount Carmel, and not in the holy city.[166]

Fragments[167]

1.

Such things[168] have often happened and still happen, and how can these be signs of the end of the world?[169]

Neumann *frag.* 3; from Julian, Book 2, derived from Cyril, Book 12. Quoted by Theodorus, bishop of Mopsuestia, in his Commentary on the New Testament. Neumann thinks that Theodorus probably wrote a refutation of Julian at Antioch about 378 A.D.

2.

Moses after fasting forty days received the law,[170] and Elijah, after fasting for the same period, was granted to see God face to face.[171] But what did Jesus receive, after a fast of the same length?[172]

Neumann *frag.* 4; from the same source as 1.

3.

And how could he lead Jesus to the pinnacle of the Temple when Jesus was in the wilderness?[173]

Neumann *frag.* 6. From the same source as 1 and 2.

4.

Furthermore, Jesus prays in such language as would be used by a pitiful wretch who cannot bear misfortune with serenity, and though he is a god is reassured by an angel. And who told you, Luke, the story of the angel, if indeed this ever happened? For those who were there when he prayed could not see the angel; for they were asleep. Therefore when Jesus came from his prayer he found them fallen asleep from their grief and he said: "Why do ye sleep? Arise and pray," and so forth. And then, "And while he was yet speaking, behold a multitude and Judas."[174] That is why John did not write about the angel, for neither did he see it.

Neumann *frag.* 7. From the same source as 3.

5.

Listen to a fine statesmanlike piece of advice: "Sell that ye have and give to the poor; provide yourselves with bags which wax not old."[175] Can anyone quote a more statesmanlike ordinance than this? For if all men were to obey you who would there be to buy? Can anyone praise this teaching when, if it be carried out, no city, no nation, not a single family will hold together? For, if everything has been sold, how can any house or family be of any value? Moreover the fact that if everything in the city were being sold at once there would be no one to trade is obvious, without being mentioned.

Neumann, *frag.* 12. From Cyril, Book 18, quoted by Photius.

6.

How did the Word of God take away sin,[176] when it caused many to commit the sin of killing their fathers, and many their children?[177] And mankind are compelled either to uphold their ancestral customs and to cling to the pious tradition that they have inherited from the ages[178] or to accept this innovation. Is not this true of Moses also, who came to take away sin, but has been detected increasing the number of sins?[179]

Not in Neumann; reconstructed by him from the polemical writings of Archbishop Arethas of Caesarea who wrote in refutation of Julian in the tenth century. First published by Cuinont, *Recherches sur la tradition manuscrite de l'empereur Julien*, Brussels, 1898. Neumann's reconstruction is in *Theologische Litteraturzeitung*, 10. 1899.

7.

The words that were written concerning Israel[180] Matthew the Evangelist transferred to Christ,[181] that he might mock the simplicity of those of the Gentiles who believed.

Notes

Cf. Gregory Nazianzen, *First Invective Against Julian* 76 (115), Γαλιλαίυς ἀντὶ Χριστιανῶν ὀνομάσας καὶ καλεῖσθαι νομοθετήσας. This was ignored by Neumann in his reconstruction of the work, which he entitled Κατὰ Χριστιανῶν. Cf. Socrates 3. 12.

1. *John* 7. 52.
2. In the fragmentary *Letter* 55, *To Photinus*, p. 189.
3. Libanius, in his *Monody on Julian*, says that at Antioch there were composed by the Emperor βιβλίων συνγγραφαὶ βοηθούντων θεοῖς; in the *Epitaph on Julian*, that the attack on Christian doctrines was composed in the long nights of winter, i.e. 362-363, at Antioch, where he spent the winter with Julian.
4. Geffcken, *Zwei Griechische Apologeten*, p. 250, speaks of a Chinese polemic against Christianity, composedaccording to the regular conventions of this type.
5. On Julian's debt to Porphyry, and his lack of sympathy with Porphyry's attitude to religion, see Harnack, *Porphyrius*, Berlin, 1916 ; Bidez, *Vit de Porphyre*, Gand, 1913.
6. *Oration* 18. 178.
7. For a full discussion of the work of Cyril and the other Christian apologists who attempted to refute Julian, and for an explanation of Neumann's method of reconstruction, the reader is referred to the Latin *Prolegomena* to Neumann's Edition of Julian's polemic. The numerous passages or expressions in this treatise that can he paralleled in Julian's other works have been collected by Asmus in his Concordance, Julian's *Galiläerschrift*, 1904.
8. The marginal numbers in Neumann's text represent the paging of the edition of Cyril by Spanheim, 1696, as rearranged by Neumann. In the Introduction to his edition he defends his rearrangement of the text of Aubert 1638, given by Spanheim.
9. Some words are lost.
10. Cf. *Oration'* 6. 183C, Vol. 2.
11. Cyril 70a ridicules Julian for confusing here a god with a throne; but καὶ can be interpreted "or."
12. Persephone.
13. Hades.
14. *Genesis* 2. 18.
15. *Genesis* 3. 22.
16. For Julian's belief that myths need allegorical interpretation cf. *Oration* 5. 169-170, Vol. 1, p. 475, note; see also *Caesars* 306C, *Oration* 7. 206C, 220, for myths as emblematic of the truth. This is the regular method of Neo-Platonic writers, such as Sallustius, in dealing with the unpleasant or incongruous elements in Greek mythology.
17. The pagan theory is missing and also part of the Jewish, according to Asmus.
18. In his *Letter to a Priest* 292, Vol. 2, Julian contrasts the Platonic account of the Creation with the Mosaic.
19. *Numbers* 12. 8: "With him will I speak mouth to mouth."
20. *Genesis* 1-17, with certain omissions.
21. *Timaeus* 28B, C.
22. *Timaeus* 30B; cf. Julian, *Oration* 5. 170D.
23. *Genesis* 26. 27, 28.
24. *Timaeus* 41a,b,c. Julian may have been quoting from memory, as there are omissions and slight variations from our text of the *Timaeus*.
25. Cf. Julian, Vol. 1, *Oration* 4. 149a, 156d.
26. Julian's Fourth *Oration*, Vol. 1. is an exposition of this theory held by the late Neo-Platonists; in the present treatise he does not, as in the Fourth and Fifth *Orations*, distinguish the intelligible (νοητοί) gods from the intellectual (νοεροί).
27. *Deuteronomy* 4. 19: "And lest . . . when thou seest the sun and the moon and the stars, even all the host of heaven, thou be drawn away and worship them, and serve them, which the Lord thy God hath divided unto all the peoples under the whole heaven."
28. *Exodus* 4. 22.
29. *Exodus* 4. 23.

30. *Exodus* 5. 3: the sayings of Jesus and the prophets, which Julian said he would quote, are missing.
31. For this proverb, derived from Theognis, cf. *Misopogon* 349d, Vol. 2
32. *Romans* 3. 29; *Galatians* 3. 28.
33. Psalms 78. 25.
34. *Exodus* 20. 5.
35. In *Misopogon* 359b Julian speaks of the fierceness of the Celts compared with the Romans.
36. A Scythian prince who travelled in search of knowledge and was counted by some among the seven sages. On his return to Thrace he is said to have been killed while celebrating the rites of Cybele, which were new to the Scythians; Herodotus 4. 76, tells the tale to illustrate the Scythian hatred of foreign, and especially of Greek, customs; cf. Lucian, Anacharsis.
37. He means the Gauls and Iberians, since the Germans at that time were distinguished only in warfare.
38. *Genesis* 11. 4-8.
39. *Odyssey* 11. 316.
40. Cf. *Oration* 4, 140a, Vol. 1, on the creative gods.
41. Cf. *Oration* 4. 141b, note, and 145c, note; Plato, *Laws* 713d.
42. A few words are lost.
43. i.e. if there were to be differences of speech and political constitution, they must have been adapted to pre-existing differences of nature in human beings.
44. *Genesis* 11. 7. "Go to, let us go down, and there confound their language." . . . The word "us" has been variously interpreted.
45. *Exodus* 20. 2-3.
46. *Exodus* 20. 4.
47. *Exodus* 20. 13-17.
48. *Deuteronomy* 4. 24; *Hebrews* 12. 29.
49. According to Cyril's summary, Julian next reproaches the Christians for having forsaken the Greek doctrines about God.
50. e. in the Greek accounts of the gods; probably Julian refers to Plato and a phrase to this effect may have dropped out at the beginning of the sentence.
51. *Numbers* 25. 11.
52. According to Cyril, Julian then argued that the Creator ought not to have given way so often to violent anger against and even wished to destroy, the whole Jewish people.
53. A reference to Hermes Trismegistus, "thrice greatest Hermes," whom the Greeks identified with the Egyptian god Thoth. The Neo-Platonists ascribed certain mystic writings to this legendary being and regarded him as a sage.
54. A Babylonian fish-god described by Berosus in his *History of Babylonia*. He was supposed to have taught the Chaldaeans the arts of civilisation and has some analogy with the serpent of *Genesis*.
55. This is the Greek version of the Assyrian *bil*, "lord" or "god," the Baal of the Bible.
56. The Centaur who taught Achilles.
57. According to Cyril's summary, Julian then ridicules David and Samson and says that they were not really brave warriors, but far inferior to the Hellenes and Egyptians, and their dominion was very limited.
58. Cf. *Oration* 4. 156c, the Hellenes perfected the astronomy of the Chaldaeans and Egyptians.
59. They had discovered the laws of musical intervals.
60. According to Cyril, Julian then related stories about Minos, and the myth of Dardanus, the account of the flight of Aeneas, his emigration to Italy and the founding of Rome.
61. i.e. Rome.
62. Numa Pompilius, a legendary king who is supposed to have succeeded Romulus; various portents manifested the favour of the gods towards Numa. Cf. Julian, *Oration* 4. 155a, note, Vol. 1.
63. A few words are missing.

64. A small shield, *ancile*, on whose preservation the power of Rome was supposed to depend, was said to have fallen from the sky in Numa's reign. Livy 1. 20 refers to it in the plural, *caelestia arma quae ancilia appellantur*; cf. also *Aeneid* 8. 664, *lapsa ancilia coelo*.

65. When the foundations were dug for the temple of Jupiter a human head, *caput*, was found; this was regarded as an omen, and hence the Capitoline Hill received its name; cf. Livy 1. 55. For Julian's belief in such traditions cf. *Oration* 5. Vol. 1, 161b on the legend of Claudia and the image of Cybele.

66. Here Cyril retorts that Julian admired what others condemn, e.g. the cruel and superstitious Marius, who, said he, was given to the Romans by the gods. The worship of Cybele was another gift from heaven to Rome. Julian then referred to various kinds of divination.

67. Julian is thinking of the oracle of Delphi which he had in vain endeavoured to restore.

68. i.e. of divination by entrails and other omens.

69. See Vol. 1, Introduction to *Oration* 4, p. 349; and for Asclepius, *Oration* 4. 144b, where Julian, as here, opposes Asclepius to Christ; and 153b for Asclepius the saviour.

70. The martyrs.

71. Cf. *Misopogon* 361b, Vol. 2.

72. For the massacres of heretics by the Christians cf. Julian's letter *To the Citizens of Bostra*, p. 129.

73. Jesus Christ; cf. above, 194d.

74. *Acts* 10, the story of Cornelius the centurion.

75. *Acts* 13. 6-12; Sergius was the proconsul.

76. See above 201 e.

77. *Exodus* 6. 6.

78. *Judges* 2. 16.

79. 1 *Samuel* 8.

80. *Luke* 2. 2.

81. *Ezekiel* 3, 7.

82. *Mark* 1. 27.

83. Eusebius, *Praeparatio Evangelica* 11. 5. 5 says that Moses and David wrote in "the heroic metre."

84. 1 *Kings* 11. 4: "His wives turned away his heart after other gods." Julian may allude to Pharaoh's daughter, see 1 *Kings*, 3. 1.

85. Julian seems to refer to the saints

86. 1 *Corinthians* 8. 7-13.

87. Some words are missing. The summary of Cyril shows that Julian next attacked the Old Testament and ridiculed it because it is written in Hebrew.

88. Cf. 43b.

89. παρυφή, Latin *clavus*, is the woven border of a garment.

90. Cf. *Deuteronomy* 32. 9.

91. *Exodus* 22. 28.

92. Cf. 314c and *Oration* 6. 192d, Vol. 2, where he quotes with a sneer "these words of the Galilaeans," from *Genesis* 9. 3.

93. Cf. *Letter* 36 for Julian's reproach against the Christian rhetoricians that they behave like hucksters.

94. 1 *Corinthians* 6. 9-11.

95. In Cyril's summary, Julian next compares the Christian converts with slaves who run away from their masters in the belief that, even if they do not succeed in escaping, their state will be no worse than before.

96. *Acts* 3. 22; *Deuteronomy* 18. 18.

97. *Genesis* 49. 10.

98. Or "whose it is"; Julian follows the Septuagint. The version "until Shiloh come" was not then current; cf. Skinner, *Genesis*, p. 522. It is still debated whether these words refer to the Davidic kingdom or to a future Messiah, and there is no universally accepted rendering of the Hebrew original.

99. Cf. *Matthew* 1. 1-17 with *Luke* 3. 23-38.
100. Cyril's reply to this part of Julian's Second Book is lost, so that the Emperor's more detailed discussion cannot be reconstructed.
101. *John* 1.3.
102. *Numbers* 24. 17.
103. *Deuteronomy* 4. 35.
104. *Deuteronomy* 4. 39.
105. *Deuteronomy* 6. 4.
106. *Deuteronomy* 32. 39.
107. *John* 1. 1.
108. The heretical bishop Photinus of Sirmium was tried under Constantius before the synod at Milan in 351 for denying the divinity of Christ; see Julian's letter to him, p. 187.
109. *Isaiah* 7. 14.
110. *John* 1. 18.
111. *Colossians* 1. 15.
112. *John* 1. 3.
113. A paraphrase of *Isaiah* 26. 13.
114. *Isaiah* 37. 16.
115. Apparently a paraphrase of *Deuteronomy* 32. 39.
116. *Genesis* 6. 2.
117. *Genesis* 6. 4.
118. *Exodus* 4. 22.
119. *Deuteronomy* 6. 13.
120. *Matthew* 28. 19.
121. According to Cyril's summary, Julian says that the Hellenes, unlike the Christians, observe the same laws and customs as the Jews, except that they worship more than one god and practise soothsaying. Circumcision is approved by the temple priests of Egypt, the Chaldaeans and Saracens. All alike offer the various sorts of sacrifice, including those for atonement and purification. Moses sacrificed to the abominable deities who avert evil, the *di averrunci*.
122. A paraphrase of *Leviticus* 16. 5-8.
123. "Mercy-seat" is the usual version.
124. *Leviticus* 16. 15.
125. *Leviticus* 7. 20.
126. Cf. 43a.
127. Sozomen 5. 22, Socrates 3. 20 and Theodoret 3. 15 relate that Julian summoned the leading Jews and exhorted them to resume their sacrifices. Their reply that they could lawfully sacrifice only in the Temple led him to order its restoration.
128. According to Cyril, Julian then says that the Christians in worshipping not one or many gods, but three, have strayed from both Jewish and Hellenic teaching.
129. Cf. 238d, note.
130. *Acts* 10. 15.
131. *Leviticus* 11. 3.
132. *i.e.* of the Galilaeans.
133. *Exodus* 12. 14-15; Julian went on to quote several similar passages from the Old Testament, but these are missing.
134. *Romans* 10. 4.
135. "The gods, not being ignorant of their future intentions, do not have to correct their errors," says Julian, *Oration* 5. 170a,
136. *Deuteronomy* 4. 2.
137. *Deuteronomy* 27, 26, "Cursed be he that confirmeth not all the words of this law to do them." Cf. *Galatians* 3. 10.
138. According to Cyril, Julian next discussed the letter of the Apostles to the Christian converts, and, quoting *Acts* 15. 28, 29, which forbid the eating of meats offered to idols and things strangled, says that this does not mean that the Holy Ghost willed that the Mosaic law

should be disregarded. He ridicules Peter and calls him a hypocrite, convicted by Paul of living now according to Greek, now Hebrew, customs.

139. For Christianity a disease cf. *Oration* 7. 229d, and *Letter* 58 *To Libanius* 401c.
140. *John* 1. 14.
141. *John* 1. 18.
142. *John* 1. 19.
143. Yet in *Letter* 47. 434c, Julian reproaches the Alexandrians with worshipping as God the Word "one whom neither you nor your fathers have ever seen, even Jesus."
144. *i.e.* that Jesus was God.
145. For the collection of the "bones and skulls of criminals," and the apotheosis of the martyrs as it struck a contemporary pagan, see Eunapius, *Lives* p. 424 (Loeb edition). Julian, in *Letter* 22. 429d, commends the Christian care of graves; here he ridicules the veneration of the relics of the martyrs, which was peculiarly Christian and offensive to pagans.
146. For this phrase, derived from Plato, *Phaedo* 81d, cf. *Misopogon* 344a. Eunapius, *Lives* p. 424 προσεκαλινδοῦντο τοῖς μνήμασι, of the Christian worship at the graves of the martyrs.
147. *Matthew* 23. 27.
148. According to Cyril, Julian quoted *Matthew* 8. 21, 22: "Let the dead bury their dead," to prove that Christ had no respect for graves.
149. In part from *Isaiah* 65. 4; the literal meaning of the Hebrew is "that sit in graves and pass the night in secret places," a reference to incubation for the sake of dream oracles, a Hellenic custom. Julian professes to believe that this practice, which Isaiah abhorred, was kept up by the Christians.
150. *Leviticus* 9. 24.
151. 1 *Kings* 18. 38.
152. Cyril says that Julian told the story of the interrupted sacrifice of Isaac by Abraham from *Genesis* 22.
153. *Genesis* 4. 4-7. The Hebrew text of the last sentence is corrupt, and its meaning is disputed. Skinner, *Genesis,* p. 106, calls the Septuagint version, followed by Julian, fantastic.
154. *Genesis* 4. 3-4.
155. This was, perhaps, Aetius, for whom see p. 289.
156. An allusion to *Romans* 4. 11-12 and 2. 29.
157. A paraphrase of *Genesis* 17. 10-11; according to Cyril, Julian quoted *Matthew* 5. 17, 19, to prove that Christ did not come to destroy the law.
158. *i.e.* Christ.
159. Cf. *Genesis* 17. 13.
160. This is a sneer rather than an argument.
161. Cf. *Letter* 20, *To Theodorus,* 454a, where Julian says that the Jewish god "is worshipped by us under other names."
162. *Genesis* 24. 2, 10, 43, foll. This was Eleazar. Maimonides the Jewish jurist, writing in the twelfth century, says, "One who sets signs for himself . . . like Eleazar the servant of Abraham," with reference to *Genesis* 24. 14. The epithet συμβολικὸς is probably a translation of the Hebrew. I am indebted for this note to Professor Margoliouth.
163. Partly paraphrased from *Genesis* 15. 1-6.
164. Cyril says that Julian then asserted that he himself had been instructed by omens from birds that he would sit on the throne.
165. 1 *Kings* 18. 19.
166. Only the fragments which preserve the actual words of Julian are here given; several of Neumann's are therefore omitted.
167. *e.* wars, famines, etc.
168. Cf. *Matthew* 24. 3-14.
169. *Exodus* 31. 18.
170. 1 *Kings* 19. 9.
171. *Matthew* 4. 2, foll.
172. *Matthew* 4. 5.
173. *Luke* 22. 42-47.

174. *Luke* 12. 33.
175. Julian is criticising St. John's Gospel, as he criticised its prologue in *Against the Galilaeans,* Book 1. He attacks *John* 1. 29; cf. *John* 1. 3. 5.
176. *Matthew* 10. 21. "And the brother shall deliver up the brother to death, and the father the child; and the children rise up against their parents, and cause them to be put to death."
177. He means that in this case too their sins have not been taken away by the Word, since they remain heathens.
178. *In Leviticus* 16. Aaron is to make atonement for the sins of Israel, but the severe Mosaic law increased the opportunities for transgression.
179. *Hosea* 11. 1. "When Israel was a child, then I loved him and called my son out of Egypt."
180. *Matthew* 2. 15. "That it might be fulfilled which was spoken of the Lord by the prophet, saying, 'Out of Egypt have I called my son.'"